CW01496520

The Light
of
Jesus

*A simple guide of truth, spiritual philosophy and wisdom
as given by Jesus and the Christ realm.*

by

RoseAnne Rosslin

The Light of Jesus
by
RoseAnne Rosslin

www.roseannerosslin.com
info@roseannerosslin.com

Paperback ISBN: 978-1-9164735-0-8
E-book ISBN: 978-1-9164735-1-5

Dedication

This book is dedicated to all.

As I slept He watched over me
As I woke He offered me
These words to give
For man to take
In love, light
And purity.

There is no right
There is no wrong
There only Is
In unity.

Contents

CHAPTER 2

CHAPTER 3

CHAPTER 4

The Light of the Truth   85

CHAPTER 5

The Light of the Rose 99

EPILOGUE

An Introduction from the Christ Realm

This book has come through the channel RoseAnne on behalf of the Christ realm. We are eternally grateful to our channel for relaying our message to the world. It is not our intention to provoke or upset any person with this knowledge but to bring love and peace, light and joy and most of all growth to mankind.

It is time for the truth of your beloved Jesus to be fully known that he came to the Earth world to progress the spirit of man, to unfold kindness, to uplift man's heart and teach you to respect yourselves and All That Is.

If you should find the truth difficult to acknowledge, then let it go. This book brings fresh knowledge to your world and it is the truth, it is simple and it is.

These words have been faithfully transcribed from the Christ realm and collated over a twenty-year period. It is now we bring these words through RoseAnne to awaken man's spirituality further into new realms, to heighten his awareness, to strengthen his spiritual cord and to give him hope. Hope of himself, hope of the future. Hope brings clarity, a strong determined word to bind the focus, a target, a knowing. Hope is a now word, it brings light and brightness, raises the spirit and in turn the consciousness to allow others to help on your lifepaths journey. Focus is key to determine the spirits activity.

The human consciousness is growing in power and needs the assistance of the higher realms to gather its muscle, to strengthen the way, to channel the energy in the direction of good and greatness for all, so be it.

A Note from RoseAnne

I am the scribe, I am 'the writer'.

The words given to me by the Christ realm are delivered in short and concise sentences with rhetorical questions which I annotate literally on behalf of Spirit. The channellings come in different forms of language, some general, some biblical, some modern day; a colour spectrum of energy that makes up the Christ realm.

Mankind is often referred to in general as man and men. The few words written in brackets I have added, to bring the reader further clarity on the channelled text.

Chapter 1

The Light of Jesus

My Words

These words have been brought to the channel from a very special place in the Spirit world. The channel has prepared these words with love for you all to read knowing she has exercised her ability to listen to the truth and scrutinise the word of Spirit.

These are my words, Jesus.

The True Word of Love

In a time of turmoil and injustice, I could not have had a harder task than bringing out the spirit of man. Men were philosophers or tradesman or surviving with little trade or skill. I had not the books to tell my fellow men where the chakras lay or the spirit existed. It came through experience. Experience of the heart, the bloodshed, the turmoil and strife.

You cannot see how much easier it is for you, as people have some knowledge through literature and the media of spiritual existence. Man is not ignorant of the spirit, but of himself.

Many are awakened and many lie dormant and many far from the door of spiritual existence. Many have an awareness, many have communication, many give and many do God's work.

Within this book is the realisation of Spirit to assist man's awakening of his spiritual existence. One day the two (spirit and physical) will integrate like shopping on the internet. If you wanted to look up your Aunty in Spirit it will be possible for each soul to connect. No cost, no medium, the means of transport is within himself. If you require spiritual knowledge or wisdom it will be given.

Spiritual love has yet to truly unfold. It is being misused. You are aware of the sensitive souls who cannot handle true love without fault, without conditions, without delusions. It is time to spread the true word of love.

My story continues.

The Christ Light

The realm of Christ.
The light of Christ for all man and more.
The healing light of Christ.
The miraculous light of Christ.

'The missing chapter: His wife and life as a married blessed man, His children, no names, no record, no knowledge. The purity of Jesus kept intact for politics'.

'This knowledge is not new, it is out there in the books and men's minds. But what if we told you He didn't die on the cross. He was beaten to death and placed upon the cross. His life has become a spectacle'.

I come to teach the many to truly love one another, to give of yourself in light, in truth, not to win awards or prizes but to recognise the need of men within you and the group. The growing intention to live as one is misguided, the intention is to be as one and to live in your light then the light of others will shine.

The infestation and disease of man is not the will of God. The God light is shining on the corruption of the planet. The reverence, the holy are losing power as man recognises his individuality, his expression of the light in him.

No church can bring this, it can offer solace to the heart, peace to the mind but the God light comes from within, a fact now known by man but man still searches randomly within.

Those that are enlightened are truly few. Those that can sense the God light are many. Those that can hear God are few.

This will now increase. The joy of God's light will emanate on Earth. The planet will lighten and the Spirit world will enter the Earth world. The integration is already taking place.

My place in history will be replaced by another far greater than me and man will bow down in honour, humbled by the light this man brings. A time, beyond time. A time of truth and respect, love and light, peace and glory, honour.

Honour of oneself.
Honour in all things.
Honour in the union of man with God.

Light in Our Souls

Light in our souls, the very essence of our being. The spark within can be more easily found through knowledge, literature, following steps to feel the spark. But what if you are not meant to be aware till the moment you feel the spark for yourself. What if you cannot really feel the light and sit there only visualising from instructions in a book. Is this right or is this wrong? Is it good to know or better to feel? Is it great to know and then learn to feel? How can you know?

For those who are lost amongst the sea of literature, find your weak spot and ask that this be strengthened. Feel the light enter into your spiritual form connected by your wheels of light (chakras). Breathe in the light and out the love. Your soul will respond to the earthly consciousness. The weak spot will be found and enriched. The body will be lightened. The help will be there, but you must trust more than ever before that you are helped. You are given the tools by man but the trigger is spirit. It enlightens your soul.

Your weak spot is fallible. Your weak spot is knowing your self within. The part that no one sees, the hidden treasure. The gift you have been bestowed lying dormant in the soul.

Unload your burdens to see your soul within. Breathe in the light in solitude to hear the voice within. Take out the I and bring in the we. Feel the universal love, the connection of spirit. The knowing you are not alone.

The Divine is Simple

A personality is important and unimportant. The divine is simple.

The characters add spice to the ingredients. Man in flesh. It is divine. It is beautiful and joyous. Enjoy the flesh. Treasure the temple. Care and nurture your house of the spirit. It is with you for a short time. The spirit is eternal. This body will seep back into the earth's soil when you have finished this lifetime.

Why seek only for spirit? Look after the house. Lay each foundation stone again with light. Rebuild, renew and rejuvenate your body. It is precious and worthy of your spirit. Value your body. Value your character that is moulded within this chosen vessel. Value your personality. Acknowledge how man portrays his beauty or darkness and know each is right for each man's lessons.

How can you see beyond the characters of the evolved spirit as one if you do not look at your fellow men as one? What is one?

One is the unity of love.
One is the unity of wisdom.
One is the divine.
The oneness, the whole.

There is no singular of spirit, there is no plural of spirit. There is spirit. Each connected, interconnected, divided, multiplied and many to make one recipe from many ingredients. The milk of life.

There is no separation in Spirit and it can be more easily and readily felt. There is separation on Earth with the physical vessel. It is a pure form of transport for the spirit to travel on a planet that is so far removed from its homeland, until the moment it awakens and sees within the dense fog of darkness, the light inside. The 'God inside of me'.

Time, space, travel all searched far outside of this vessel. Millions and millions of pounds spent on this venture. How much do you pay for your fare to Spirit? What is the price you have paid to find your magic carpet?

Man searches for the spirit within when loneliness, desolation, pain, unfulfillment, boredom or inquisitiveness eats at his soul, looking for answers. Then the sad emotions turn to joy, elation, celebration, beauty, the whole, unity, oneness and many spirits gather to assist in the soul's journey to expand the consciousness of man.

Look for the light of each soul, the beauty in each spirit, the shining personality and unique character of the man. With these laws you cannot make mistakes. As you give you will receive, as you receive you shall give. This is your kingdom on Earth. Bring the kingdom of your Heaven to Earth.

Love, Light and Harmony

In my time on Earth, I gave thanks continually for the good, the bad, indifferent, all energy.

I gave homage to the people, the farmers, the carpenters, the blacksmiths, the cooks, the children, the mothers and wives.

All the people were my people. I knew their hearts, I knew their song. I gave out light to all.

My duty is light which is love and I gave out this light to all.

Can you do the same? Can the people follow me? Follow my example. Can they remember this? Keep it close to their hearts.

Let the mind clear and bring in the light. Control the mind. Take reign over their emotions.

Accept each other. Live in harmony. Start with the harmony of you. The song of the self.

It is most important to be yourself. Express you as you.

The Mind

There are two minds. Your own individual mind and the mind of God, the divine mind.

There is a third mind, the collective consciousness of man.

The higher mind is the super conscious self, the spirit of you.

The mind is split into different levels of consciousness. There are different parts of the 'you' mind.

The conscious mind is the working mind. Keep this clear, clarity is key. Let the emotions untangle from this mind. It is the working mind that thinks, not the feeling mind of the heart.

Sometimes a man can be corrupt or misunderstood as his working mind is diseased, shortened. It doesn't have the capability of a good working mind.

Others bypass this mind and use more of their higher powers. They can naturally tap into the divine mind and seek the answers, the knowings and the creativity with clarity. Man is predominantly the mind; the rest is matter.

Some have no mind and are known for their light. Their existence alone is what matters and they give out the light to the whole.

If you could understand the creation of man, forgiveness, love, blessings, harmony and joy would come easily.

As science progresses, man's knowledge of himself or herself must grow too. It is important that man lives in harmony with his creations and not make it his enemy. Lessons of man can create disharmony. To know thyself will help ease your lessons.

This is not a manual of how to behave, this is loving guidance to know truth of the self. My life represented truth, honesty, love, kindness and joy.

Material wealth, I was not poor. I had the riches of the earth and I knew on Earth the wealth of the spiritual kingdom, my Heaven. I walked with my guides, deities, enlightened beings of the higher realms.

All of You

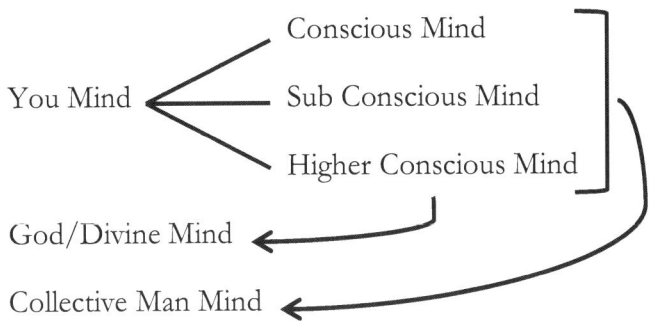

This diagram is a simple explanation of 'The Mind' as given to the channel by Spirit.

Conscious mind is the working mind of man, doing actions and earthly consciousness.

Sub Conscious mind is the deep mind of man, a collection of all earthly experiences, a memory bank to the soul.

Higher Conscious mind is the mind of spirit, the true power, connected to the power of the divine mind, All That Is.

Where is the soul? Does it have a mind? The soul is truth. Collects all in the God form. What man calls 'unconscious', we call the divine spark within the divine mind.

Create in Harmony

There is magic on the planet and beings of light that create magic. There is wonder and amazement, true love, joy, beautiful beauty and there are people creating incredulous moments, magnificent energy, sonorous sounds, blissful beauty, but one man's joy is another man's pain, one man's view is different from the next man's view.

There are more people in pain on the planet than in joy. The mental mind of the planet is at an all-time high. Man is suffering from mental fatigue as a whole. There are those that live deep in the forest, high in the mountains that know how to live with the earth and have yet to experience the world wide web, the written word. They live the old way and understand themselves individually and as a tribe better than the most learned man.

Overthinking creates havoc.
Simplicity creates nothing.
The balanced mind creates everything.

The body needs balance, the energy of the body in harmony with the planet can co-create with the masters of the Universe. There are many helping humans progress with their development and man is helping himself progress. Now there is a desire for balance, it will come too. Men will meditate, take time to relax, feed the earth, connect to their inner selves and man will enlighten.

The cut throat business world, the corporate statues will change. The unity of these organisations will deplete. Enlightened men will fill these seats, not in your lifetime will you see this change but the next.

Peace, harmony, unity, the shift, there will be a shift. Stay in the light. Fill yourself with light. Be kind. Let go of mental burdens. The mind is a great vessel for creation. Let it create harmoniously.

The Sins of Man

'He came to take away the sins of man'.

No, I did not.

The sins of man cannot be lifted by me. I can promise him to know Heaven. I can give him the light. I can show him the way. I am the way.

It is the light you seek. The light in men's hearts shine brightly or dimly. A collective consciousness can spread good or bad. Good words can lift men's hearts and spread good.

Good actions are right actions. Actions out of love. Actions out of self and lower energy does not create good. The mass can be misled to doing good and it is wrong, unhealthy and unnatural. The sins of man are his own. I didn't take the sins of man away.

There are different levels and layers of man. I led man to himself, to his good self, to be accountable for his own actions. To think aright, to think of love. To hold back the tears of hate and war. The triggers of the personality are latent feelings of frustration, boredom, ignorance.

Man takes on more than he can bear. If it is too much to burden yourself, lighten your load to be happy, live simply. Live in bliss is of highest priority than to burden oneself with duties of frustration and ignorance. Let go of the pressures that ignite the heaviest emotion, the sins that are born out of ignorance. Know thyself.

Sharing Your Gifts

The times were changing, men and women were counted for, the tax and gold was taking root in the politicians and ruler's hearts. How to manipulate the people for their own greed.

A democracy does not exist in your world. You are all owned by the Government. There is no freedom. You all have to pay taxes and those that don't, live on the edge of life or die in poverty. This world is made up of greed and although this appears harsh if you look closely enough you would know this to be true.

We want man to look more closely at himself and who surrounds him. Life on Earth is about giving of yourself, sharing your gifts, living your dream to be the best you and there are those that live their dream to obtain the best from you.

During my time on Earth I did not pay tax. I walked away from my Fathers trade to do the work of God. We were exempt. I was a leader of men and I led my men to water, food, shelter, love, family and wine. We had it all and in our communion with God we were one, united in thought, spirit and action.

Our system was based on equality. All men are equal in Gods eyes therefore all men will receive equally to what they give. Each knew their place as each felt loved, honoured and respected. The lessons for my men and women came later, on my departure and the tribe split amongst the people, the hungry people, hungry for the new, a better life and now you have luxury.

Conveniences in the household, holidays, not just at special times of the year to celebrate the earth and God's provision, now you take breaks and allow yourself time off, the worker has earned this. The technology, the equipment, the travel, the energy system, the miracles of man's mind, the science, the advancement is worthy and corrupt, eroding man's life.

I come to tell you to share your gifts, your love and your light.

Be Well

In a time of confusion and turmoil, I led my men to peace. I represented calm, kindness and love but I did not give into others emotions and I kept my own council. I kept my energy high. I listened to the command of my spirit. I knew how to be at one within my own skin and control my own emotions, they did not lead me to despair or mistrust. I guided myself to be at one with my Father in Heaven.

I could be amongst the people as I controlled me. I knew me and I responded to me, not others. Discipline of the self is living in your own energy field, not anybody else. When you feel the energy of others respond by being you. Find your energy, dismiss the energy thoughts of others.

If you feel unwell and know this not to be your energy, do all you can to be well. Being well, you in your well-being is of upmost importance. You attract the help of the wise to do this and you are supported by the positive energy we send you.

My Family

I had a wife, Mary Magdalene and I had children. I had cousins. I had family all around me. Some of you are related to me and some of you here today know me from our teaching as young boys. Some of you walked with me on part of our tours to spread the light of God. The power and energy amongst us was strong. We were a bright force and did good works. Some of you have returned to further my work and some of you know me as your brother.

My mother had many children, some lived, some died, some knew me, some didn't. We had our differences but our united faith and strong family principle kept us equal.

Our father, Joseph loved us all equally with a special hand of command and discipline. Each knew their place in the family and his word was strong. There was no violence, only peace. My father held authority, he knew himself and taught me well how to behave amongst men.

I was given the tools to lead my men. My father Joseph, knew a lot about healing men's hearts and my sister a natural born healer like me.

Our family were born to be healers. We are a healing family and anyone that desires or requires healing may ask and will be showered with our healing and led to others to give them healing. It is so.

All Stood Still

It was night time and all stood still, quiet amongst the people and we broke bread with our evening meal. It was a sanctuary, our home, a blessed house and it stood high on a hill. We were proud of our family and had plenty to eat. We sang songs and told stories and prepared for the night time to sleep. We did not wander about, we stood still along with the night calm and enjoyed each other's company.

Today it is a very different world that you live in, faster, modern, excitement, thrill and adventure. Activity, so much activity you can hardly keep still. So much to do, so little time and filled with electronic light.

Progress is wonderful, you can achieve so much without leaving your armchair but the soul needs more, it needs balance of nature, Mother Earth, Spirit and the Universal light. There needs to be time to allow the connection with the body, soul and spirit.

The Discipline of Self

Self-Discipline

The news is spreading be good, give liberally and enjoy your life but man does not ignore his own selfishness, man listens to his selfish side.

There are many making a difference and creating a new way of thinking and habits for a better world but man needs to accelerate his learning to be more disciplined with his self.

There is a large number of you co-existing on planet Earth as it provides a breeding ground of growth at all levels. Each one of you on your return to Spirit have many lessons to learn and some exceed and some super exceed and some deliver beyond measure and a few fall between the cracks, become misplaced and will return to Earth again and again and again to correct their misgivings, misdoings or enhance their growth from their previous life.

So, you think you learn your lessons only on Earth. No, there are many other places to learn and grow and Spirit is a place to develop the spirit of 'You'.

The Kingdom of Heaven

So, what does it mean the kingdom of Heaven lies within? It means your spiritual existence stems from your heart. You are connected to God through the heart of you. Your heart and mind are one. Your mind is born out of the heart.

Your physical anatomy represents your spiritual form. Your breath is God. You breathe in the God form, in Spirit, its light, on Earth its oxygen and more. Spiritual light exists on Earth. Your heart beats to keep you alive, in Spirit, it feeds you love, on Earth the blood is recycled with love.

Fill each part of your anatomy with spiritual light. See Gods light filling your lungs with light and breathe out love. Fill 'all of you' with the light of God. He is your power. He is your energy. The creative power is 'it', neither feminine nor masculine, a power connecting all of you through a ribbon of light. Fill your cells with this light and all will be well. Expand your spiritual form within you so you may grow in the light.

Stay in the light, give out the light and replenish your light and all is well.

Many Life Forms

In Spirit are many life forms. You know little of these on your planet but there are hidden life forms of great spiritual awareness and strength still to be discovered by man.

The technological age has overshadowed the growth of true spirit discovery. A new age is really coming soon where new light beings will appear on the planet Earth and walk with men of light.

Animals that do not think are filled with light descended from a great place in the sky. A source of information to man.

A New Earth

Pain follows joy or does it precede joy? Why have pain at all? Whose philosophy is this? What is Utopia? What is diversity?

The dense energy of the planet can close the mind. The higher energy of the heart can raise the energy of the planet. The planet is a being and we on the planet are here to love her and raise her, groom her and give her our light. The planet of Earth, a light star in your solar system. A beacon of light and dark, night and day. The same as man, higher and lower.

Control the forces within. Work with the forces without. Look inward to be outward. There are other life forms on other planets but man cannot reach these life forms in the state of darkness and disbelief of oneself. To know thyself.

They enter your solar system, the star men and gaze upon you with exasperation and love. A mixed race (on Earth) of colours, creed, knowledge and enlightenment and energy. How lucky you are to be rattling around together as one on a planet you disrespect.

We know there are few who are fighting for the cause of the life expansion of Earth but in the main the planet has been abused, is being misused. It has become overlooked and forsaken. The abundance of the earth will implode. A new Earth will arise.

This is not a book of doom, a book of awareness.

It's Simple

It's simple
Live in the light
Be your light
Spread your joy
Love yourself
Know who you are
Give out your light
And live in love.

Chapter 2

The Light of Mary and Joseph

Words by the Parents of Jesus

Here we give you the voices of the parents of Jesus. Their story is of great importance to let the world know the truth, the true happenings. Man has been misled to believe tales to suit the needs of those in power at the time of Jesus' existence.

For man to move forward, history is being rewritten, a new story. The words are truth, the light of Jesus came into being through Mary and Joseph, two blessed souls that remain an enigma in your world.

The Birth of Jesus

He came to me the Angel of the Lord and told me I would give birth to a baby boy and he would be called Jesus. This is true, a messenger of God visited me at night and told me I would give child to His son. He then told me it would be an easy birth and all our needs would be met.

We were wealthy which paid for His education and learning. Learning of the old ways to heal, to scribe, to live. My son Jesus came through me. The wise men provided His wealth and knowledge. He was born into kings. At the time of the birth of Jesus, it was not easy, I found it difficult amongst the chaos, the noise in the streets and towns.

Jesus was born in troubled times, a spring day, March. The birth was eased on the second visit of the Angel of the Lord and he took my angst away. He delivered the baby, the Angel being a high messenger of God and glory shone around. He released Jesus in the light.

My baby came from my womb and my husband is evidence to this, the biological father. The soul Jesus, came through me. The soul attaches itself at conception. I gave birth to Jesus, He is my physical child and God's Holy son.

The baby grew up with a family, brethren and knew love of His cousins and extended family. There was a large family around Jesus.

Many knew of his special gifts as they started easily coming in His sleep, in dreams then visions and prayer. He was visited daily by the High Priest, everyone knew He was the one that God had sent to save us all. He saved us from ourselves, taught us how to be holy or as you would term divine.

My husband blessed Him daily. He laughed a lot and brought joy to the household as well as wisdom. I was in awe of my son Jesus. He brought me many lessons.

More on the Birth of Jesus

I gave birth to Jesus at a time when the wind blew south. It was mild and the air felt pure. We were happy and yes, we did travel but we were not lost. It was a time of chaos, fighting amongst the people and destruction. But we survived above the chaos and noise, we were enlightened and guided to the right place for the birth of Jesus. It was shelter and it was dry but it was not a manger or crib for his bed, the stable was empty and there weren't any animals and you couldn't really call it a stable.

I had an accident which prematurely brought on the birth of Jesus. I was not hurt and neither was the baby. We were not too far from home but I did feel alone and away from my people. All was well and we delivered the baby easily with the help of friends. It was a time of great joy.

I tripped, the accident or pushed but I didn't hurt myself and the baby came more easily. The shock moved my waters to flow and He came soon after the fall. 'I am a mother again' I said to my husband and he danced with glee. Family was everything to us, to live a good life with those you love.

His Mother, The Blessed Virgin

Mother Mary held her baby in her arms, one day old and was proud of her son before His story had begun, as she had seen Him in her visions at night, the young man with His hands open, talking to her, helping her carry this child.

She had grown heavy and tired before giving birth to Jesus and didn't understand the fuss the learned men were making at the time of His birth. This had not been foretold to Mary but Mary knew of the importance of these men that had travelled along way to see her child, the child of God, so she ignored her fears and let these men come close to Jesus to pass on their wisdom.

Jesus was a strange child to Mary. It was as if He had been given the gift of foresight even at birth and she knew not of His impact He would make on men's hearts. Knowing He was a child of God of most high, the holiest of His children, did not give her insight of His strength and powers.

A happy child, she thought He would fit in well with the other children, her own included and He did. Jesus already had a brother and a sister and later there would be another brother. He had many cousins and He was surrounded by learned men to teach Him the other worldly ways of the spirit, to heal and create magic. He was a master, it came naturally and spoke to God every day.

His biological father known as Joseph, was a great influence upon His tribe and knew many facts and figures, earthly ways of the world and gave Jesus the grounding and trade He needed to support Him in this lifetime. Joseph was His father and He loved and respected him very much, as did all of his children including the tribe and its elders. He was a man of good values, moral truths and wisdom beyond his years. He loved Mary very much and held her in the highest esteem. His first and only lady, to him she was the blessed virgin.

His Father, The Husband

Who am I? The father of Jesus or the brother of a well-known tribe? The teacher, the rabbi and the lover of Mary. I am the husband. I have been misrepresented in your Bible as many others have and I am here to give you our truth, the truth of the Lord, to set the record straight.

I am the husband of Mary, the lover, the father, the companion. This was to be my last lifetime, my greatest work to carry the child of the true Father, the Holy one.

I was blessed and knew every day I would lose my son to the people. I was a prophet but not like you (the writer). I had insights given to me through God, I could not tap in for the answers. I was given the word only when the dove appeared and God would speak to me too telling me of my child's good, His wrong doing by man and the hurt I would endure. I was prepared for the abuse. I was unprepared for the love I felt for Jesus.

He was a blessing to all the family and He was my pride and joy. I loved all my children equally but Jesus had the special gift of truth and His truth remains to this day on Earth. Love you and all who surround you as God has placed you together to learn your lessons and grow mankind and the loving consciousness of man.

It is a gift you behold to live a lifetime on Earth. It must be loved and valued, cherished and nurtured. Be the parent of yourself and feed your soul with all you love, let God take care of the rest.

Jesus, Our Child

Our child grew up with special gifts already in place. We were honoured to be His parents. We cherished all our children but Jesus brought harmony and peace to our family. His brother James bonded with Him the most as if they were twins. Jesus led a normal life in His early years, mainly in prayer and communicating to the Heavenly Father.

Jesus was exceptional at seeing into men's hearts, their true character and helped many people onto their right paths, to make good choices for themselves and their families.

He helped people to live in their truth, to be known for their strengths, not their weaknesses. Their faults, troubles and sorrow diminished with the healing of men's hearts. He corrected their vision, their spiritual sight. He was able to see their truth and let them unfold their truth. He gave us our truth, love.

Forgiveness

To forgive, you give of yourself. It is easy in words but when the heart and mind tangles it becomes challenging to discipline yourself to believe a different situation, to another's perspective.

The mind locks and the heart turns to shame and becomes immoveable. The mind focuses on the problem and 'all of you' holds the pattern of hurt and misery surrounding the situation. To let go, to unfocus your attention, to drop it, to remove yourself from the idea seems impossible as you make it so.

Others can switch and move their minds easily out and away from the problem of hurt and discomfort and others need to grip the hurt and discomfort like a vice to remind themselves of the wrong doing and why did this happen? The lock down becomes intense, the narcissism grows like a disease and disrupts the energy of the human beings. Others suffer at the hands of the whiplash, the words run deep into their soul.

Can you forgive so easily the harm they put upon you?

No, you cannot, from where you stand you cannot see any other perspective. There is only one view and that is your own.

So, how to break this cycle, how to cut the ropes of this energetic feast, to stop the manifestation of illness and corruption within your body and soul?

Listen to the spirit of you calling to you to stop. If you cannot hear, then silence yourself. Take yourself away to be with you and ask, what do I have to learn, to give, to move forward, to heal, to bless and embrace a new me?

Not everyone wants to learn and grow and move forward. Some are happy to be miserable and give out misery and dwell on their misfortunes and some are so deeply wounded it seems impossible to clear the hatred or sadness that has grown uncontrollably within them.

We do not want the human race to suffer and hold up their growth. The injuries created are not always predestined. You have choice and you create your fate and we encourage you from the descension of Heaven to Earth to embrace your futures with love and light, but some are crooked and become mixed up, misguided in Earth's plan and a new destiny unfolds. It takes pain and many Earth years to correct the balance.

The acceleration of spiritual knowledge has activated a new growth of learning and many are ready to shed the old way, be new and reveal their truth, true character. It is a time of putting wrongs right. To forgive by giving your gifts, your light and your love you change your destiny. You become one with I am. You learn the truth about self and you recognise the light in everyone and you let go of people, objects, things, belongings and you notice the I is now 1, (one). The harm disappears, no longer a challenge, the mood lifts and the sadness disappears. The needs of the physical are met naturally and as Mary, the Mother of Jesus, truly became blessed when she forgave those that tortured and murdered her enlightened son, a man of pure morals, a ray of hope from God Himself.

It is time to forgive each other so we can all as one human race, move forward to new beginnings, to work together as one united family and the variations in each other's principles, colour, personalities and knowledge will be shared to enlighten, encourage and grow the human race. Our differences will become our strength. Embrace the differences, work with people you know you can work with, people you love and open to their viewpoints, gravitate towards your people.

The wrong doings of others are not your wrong doings. To forgive is to be free to do God's work. This is your love.

Chapter 3

The Light of Christ

Words by the Christ light

With these words are the voices of men that walked with Jesus, some you will know from your Bible and some you do not. We have not included names in all the stories as it is the stories of truth that we wish you to hear. There is a higher purpose behind the names that have been stated to bring the light of these souls forward into your time on Earth. The names are important and unimportant, but where we are, it is of no importance.

Listen to the words carefully and you will know who is reading them to you. The light of Christ, a collection of eternal beings that make up the Christ light. A name man has given to Jesus.

The Christ Realm

The Christ realm are those that have lived with Jesus, worked with Jesus and know Jesus. The Christ consciousness is made up of many. It is the light of God who is the true source of all energy, all life forms, all beings and all spiritual form of which there is many.

The God energy is in each of you and each of you has a design, a signature, an imprint to give to the world and the next.

Wherever you reside, you will learn new ways and new beginnings are always taking place. There is no end to this circle of life.

Be the Light

Jesus was born among men to give out light, be the light and raise the vibrations of the Earth, bestow knowledge to his fellow men and give out love, continual love.

He knew how to control his emotions, how to be Himself and His higher and only purpose.

Many are finding their way and many are not. Many are returning to embrace their lives to grow and seek further enlightenment, to make a difference to the planet and all that reside upon her.

The Person

The Christ light is a being. What is a being? Is it light? No, the person. There was and is a person. The person and the light are the same.

Who is the person? Jesus is the person. There is a person. You are a person. It is not to be dismissed the personality of the person.

Jesus has a personality, Jesus is a person now a spirit. The Christ light is Jesus and many others. Person applies to one, people applies to many. Jesus is part of the many but his personality shines through.

Personality is character, uniqueness of self, a representation of your soul group and your soul memories. Let your personality, the character of you shine, smile, laugh, love, live joy. Be one with who you are.

A person is born to bring life and death to the whole. The person has stories to tell, knowledge to give, light to bring, healing for all. Through him knowledge can be gained. Through the person we will start with love.

Love

Love is the golden fruit; an apple represents the forbidden fruit. Love is the answer.

Misguided love creates death, death of the soul. The unforbidden love, the greed, the controlled, the possessive love does not bear fruit and mars the soul's purpose.

True love creates life, the essence of the soul.

What is true love? Not romantic love, not possessive love. Not love for oneself (vanity).

Love like the bird that lives with nature.
Flows with the earth, exists for all time.
Bird after bird, in and out, flowing like the tide.
Rejoice in the existence of love.

Love is truly still.
Love is the air flowing through your lungs.
The rain washing your face.
These words on the page.
Love will protect and heal, heal and protect.
Love heals all and in love is the light of all.

Love can bring many lessons and teach us many things.

How to love unconditionally is a task many find difficult and for some it comes easily.

Love is truth.
Love is standing back and letting go.
Love is kindness and love is more than strength, it is.

Perfection

Perfection given to man. No, man seeks perfection. What is perfection? What is imperfection?

Is not the birth of a baby boy through toil, sweat and hardship a perfect joy? The pain brought perfection. Without the pain there cannot be perfection. Man learns from pain. If he remembers the beauty of the lessons he need not return to suffer.

But how quickly does man forget the perfect joy. When a child misbehaves, is it perfect? No, it is perfect for the child's learning. These are not riddles, this is life.

Life on Earth, primitive? No, a superior form of healing. You are brave from the start of your birth. Your journey begins with a journey of hard work. It is not easy to be born into this world. It is easier to depart. The end is not final. The end is not near. The end is not painful.

But the journey to the end can be slow and hard. A special healing of the soul comes with illness and in the soul's time the illness corrects the malfunctions the life has brought.

To prevent illness do not be at dis-ease. Be at ease.

Keep calm, stay calm and be calm.
Keep light, stay light and be happy.
Relax and enjoy your life.
We will rock you.

The Gift

As Given by Simon Peter

'The sand is bare beneath my feet and I want the grass to grow'. I teach man in Spirit how to find your oasis. When you are given a gift, a spiritual gift, you have to take care of you and treasure the gift. Sometimes you can't quite believe you have the gift. Others may want to touch and see and you may not be ready to share this gift. I don't want you to play with my gift, leave me to mine.

But what about the soul that does not have the gift? Wouldn't you say come and share with me this special gift. I can show you where you can find one like this. They could have this when they are so poor?

What do I have to give? What do I have to do?
It's simple, you say. Just open your heart.

Love all that you see from the smallest creature that looks so ugly to the most beautiful man, woman or tree and recognise and accept each for its own quality.

How do I do this when I see things I don't like, when they steal, when they abuse? And I then tell my spirit: find the God in you and you will find the God in everything. Then no man, no creature, nothing can take.

Lose the link, lose the love.
Lose the peace, lose God.
Lose trust and you are nothing.

Believe in You

Thomas didn't doubt. He lacked faith in himself. If you have faith in who you are and what you do then who needs proof, who needs evidence because your beliefs are true. Your world exists of your making and the power that surrounds you enhances your beliefs, your truths.

Jesus taught Thomas to believe in himself, to trust in his instincts, to know his beliefs. What holds you up will take you forward.

The search within, like an engineer servicing the engine of a car having taken each part out and checked it, polished it, in some cases thrown out and others put back anew.

The service is over the car is ready to run. It's ready to go far. You must know when to stop and change the oil, to re-fuel, to vanquish unwanted passengers. Be aware who surrounds you, let your spirit be protected in the light of God. The light of you to shine.

Believe in you.

Appreciation and Love

Today is as biblical as when Jesus walked the Earth. The bible is not fantasy, it is distorted and man's interpretation has distorted the truth.

The kingdom of Heaven is within each of you. Go within. Many go within wandering aimlessly.

The kingdom of Heaven is all around you. So many search within and forget to see the beauty surrounding them in all forms.

A life was given for your feet to be protected. Bless this life. Thank the life. Look for the beauty of Heaven in your home. Take time to give thanks. More can come with the appreciation and love.

Action is King

Jesus did not agree with everything man said or did. He could see beyond man's actions. He knew the soul's journey and lessons, a gift of sight not known to man. He could see into people's hearts and know the soul's journey.

Therefore, this transparency made it difficult for Jesus to be of His time. He knew their actions and consequences, He knew their truths and lies. As God knows all, so did Jesus. His own gift.

Man can change his course with his actions. His thoughts alone cannot change his actions. Action is king. Action creates change.

Knowledge Lost

Jesus came to Earth to heal mankind, to heal all life forms. Light in Him is past to us all. A great teacher, healer and knowledgeable soul. His teachings are simple, be kind, be loving, be knowing, be all to others as you would to yourself but man has lost self-love.

To love yourself is to honour the divine energy within you. How to love oneself? Love thyself. What does it mean to love thyself?

It means honour the spirit housed in your body. It feels trapped unable to do the things it can do in the Spirit world. Like a child learning to move, draw, paint, play music, any art form, the spirit has to adjust to the shape and form of the body you have chosen. The spirit needs freedom and you are restricted. It now has a brain to move the body, a thinking part. It needs cherished as all the organs do as each has a specific function with your spirit.

The spirit is enlightened. The spirit should govern the body not the brain. The brain is an entity. The spirit is one with the universal mind of All That Is. It is impossible for you to understand the spirit's freedom from your perspective. The spirit is All That Is.

A Witness on the Mountain

A View from Peter

The mountain stood high above the hills, view was magnificent, felt near to God. The air clear and pure. How I liked the atmosphere, it was saintly. Cleansed of all sins.

The mountain had been prepared by Jesus. The Earth's atmosphere lifted to the universal energies higher than our own. Communication with spirit clear. The vibrations raised. He raised the Earth's atmosphere. People entered into the boundaries of God.

The words seemed irrelevant compared to the atmosphere. Power amongst us. Not all felt the power. You could feel the power. The light was pouring through into our souls, cleansing, healing. The words floated over. For those nearer Earth, the words meant more and played their part, powerful words.

Energy comes in many forms. You can feel, hear, sense, speak, see, touch all your senses come to life.

Raise your soul. Soul, spirit, body. Renew your soul. Remember your soul's purpose. Give yourself life.

The life of Jesus was precious. Words He spoke remembered years later, but the energy needs to be remembered. How can we describe the feeling that entered our hearts? He brought the magnificence to Earth. Tap into the energy of the mountain. It remains, it exists.

He brought together humanity. A small gathering to be healed and carry the seeds of goodness. It is in you all. Carry it forward. Let the seed grow.

The goodness is kindness.
The goodness is love.
The goodness is being.

Field of Love and Passion

From the Aunt of Jesus, Mother Mary's Sister

When Jesus was flogged by the Romans the pain was greater in men's hearts that knew Christ, the Holy Spirit. Men suffered more than Jesus. They took His pain from His flesh into their own hearts leaving Him without energy.

Let men suffer their own pain as their energy heals and protects them. It is not given to man to take away God's laws from another.

Who took Jesus' pain from Him? Who suffered on His behalf? Who is suffering now on His behalf? Carrying the pain and torture of another man is wrong.

The crucifix is a sign of suffering for some and others remember His love. For others, it's meaningless embellishment. There are sanctuaries of suffering on Earth, churches of misdeeds, unhealthy living, ignorance.

Bring in the field of love and passion. Life is for living not dying. The field of love and passion. The field is God's Earth. Those that love life, love Christ in themselves. Those that have turned their back on the love of life, you must not follow their path. You cannot take their pain away. You cannot live their pain and suffering. It is not for you to carry the hearts of men.

Sending love and light to others is the right thing to do and bring light to their spiritual eyes.

Do not abandon man in his pain, but love him more.

Bring in the Light

The Roman

Death of Christ. I killed Christ. The flesh was warm. The times were hard. We had to obey. The orders were strong. I could not leave my rank. My choice was limited. Opportunities did not seem abundant. You have abundance in opportunities.

Life is not about killing the spirit or denying the flesh. No more darkness. Bring in the light. Let go of the pain. Bring in the many. Re-organise your house. The house of God. Re-live your actions. Actions of good and plenty. Abuse of Christ's body after death. Don't abuse the body in life.

What did Christ want to teach? Is love the way? Is purity the way? Is love and kindness the same? How do you teach love? Where the heart has turned cold what will melt the hurt, the pain, the coldness?

Christ the unknown entity, the records hidden, destroyed, mutilated and undiscovered. But in the heart of every man lies the Christ light, the God light, the light of All That Is.

The Christ light is the God light. Man is of God. What is God? God Is, an energy so potent no man could describe, the life exists and is in all.

Light is All That Is needed. What is light? Light comes in many forms in a smile, in kindness, in laughter, in joy, in love. Thoughts of higher vibrations spread light. There are those that can meditate and spread light from their heart, connect with higher forces and give out light. There are those that can do great acts of kindness and there are those that can simply be and give out light.

In every walk of life there are men and women that are bright forces of nature. It comes natural to their being to be bright.

Those that are in need or suffer great loss or pain benefit from the balance brought to Earth of those that deliver only light. Hidden gems amongst the people, the people of light that walk the Earth in silence to bring balance and uplift the planetary alignment.

Be conscious in light. Live in your higher conscious and bring in the light.

All is Eternal

In the beginning, the word.

There is no beginning and there is no end, all is eternal. In eternity we live no matter what shape or form, we live. The word is good and here are the words: Heaven is a time space reality. Your thinking is crooked.

There is no separation, even now people separate physical from non-physical reality. Reality is a word of no use to us. There is no reality, only illusion and more illusion. What you believe, it is.

Who is God? All That Is. No, God is more. The more of you, the more of life, the beyond.

Is it out of reach? It is. You separate from us to be you and return to the more to be it.

How to stop the separation and be enlightened? To be light, to join your energy with All That Is and more and be it.

What do you believe? If belief is a thought then what do you think?

If you doubt then you do not believe. If you believe then create what you desire.

Is there karma? Of course. How to overcome karma? How to work through karma? How to accept your karma, embrace the lifetimes of past to this, is it relevant? Of course.

So, how do you achieve All That Is and more and create the most joyous lifetime? It's easy.

Focus the mind, be true to the heart. Speak only words that flow the truth and control your thoughts. The actions will not suffer but broaden your horizons, the actions become accurate and strong. Inspired action is true thought, be true to your purpose.

Know your purpose, it's not a wish, it's the extension of source, All That Is and more. You can do it by slowing down. Be slow at work. Be thoughtful always. Be mindful continually. Relax the mind with spirit, join forces with your higher power and be the truth.

When you are very weary of trying, try no longer. Do not try anything but only do when you know to do. Only be until you know to do, only do what you know to be.

Healing in these words, healing in your actions, healing is going slow. When life goes too fast and absorbs your power then stop. Do not go any further.

You must stop to re-evaluate, to regain and replenish. If you feel weary, sleep or rest, but know you always have energy. If you feel without it will be, so replenish.

Let go of what is on your mind, it is not on ours. A conscious thought of action to cook tea, to hang the washing out, to fill the car with petrol etc. etc. are just actions of must do, when to do, how to do.

A subconscious thought is an alive thought buried deep in the mind, she did that, I wish I had, if only I could, wouldn't it be nice, please let me have, remember when, it never did, it always has. Memories, a database, a filing cabinet of earthly experiences, a memory bank to the soul.

The superconscious mind is the true power, the power of the greater universal divine mind, the daddy of computers, the mind you will never comprehend in your physical perspective. The 'Grand Mind' is the most beautiful programme. Be the software and run with the programme, write your own notes in this programme.

So, let's start, shall I do this or shall I do that. No, that's not how it works. You wait till the divine mind speaks. Each and every action has to come from a knowing.

The Christ-mas

What a time to celebrate the birth of Jesus. Nonsense. Man has made nonsense out of this time, all religions, all faiths and all non-believers but it is a time to celebrate and share gifts with those you love and like. It is a time to recognise the birth of Christ to remember a great soul and be kind and loving to each other and it is wonderful to see man celebrate his self with others, but it has a dark side.

Crime rises, poverty heightens and stress becomes automatic and allowed. There are those that have control of this, do not react and take control of their emotions and there are those that are caught up in each other's dramas that they forget themselves.

We recommend no Christmas but a time of thanks giving. A time to give to those who are in desperate need and to ask that the Universal light spreads amongst them and to remember Jesus' love, to heal and honour oneself in an act of kindness.

The glamour and glitz has corrupted the truth. The people have moved away from their truth to celebrate a tree, presents and food. It is good to celebrate, bring love and light and family together but the emphasis is on the man-made light.

The tunes, the fun, the merriment, the joy, the love, the gifts, the sharing could all take place if stripped back to the truth which it shall be when over indulgence is at its all-time high, when the market place is saturated all year with Christmas. The change will come, it will swing to the poor, cut backs, over spending. Drowning in sorrow is not man's pleasure.

Letting Go

Good Friday

Dying, giving up, letting go, putting down the cross, saying goodbye, leaving behind, looking forward, seeing beyond, throw your eyes, letting in the divine.

A process of giving up the old and letting in the new given to man by a holy and sacred spirit, Jesus. His journey on Earth was short in years but long in wisdom and filled with joy every day.

In the morning He blessed himself, others, friends and asked for these blessings in communion with His Father in Spirit, 'the Great Spirit'.

A time of sorrow came for others at His departure from this world, His death, His leaving behind the body of His spirit.

What do you leave behind today? What will you let go of? And what are your blessings from the Father in Spirit? Who do you ask to be blessed? Who will bring those blessings?

Life is a journey of expectations. The solitude of the spirit defines these expectations. Give us today our daily bread. What do you expect to come your way in life?

Can others fill your heart with love? Do you expect them to give you their love?

Expect the love that is within you and each of us to blossom through others.

Let them be your mentor for life's journey.
Let the flower unfold to the sun.
Let the petals slowly open so you can see inside.

There is Only Life

Easter Sunday

The Christ light is upon us. It never stops shining. The light is made up of the God light.

The God light is the Christ light. The Christ light is an entity. It is made up of many souls, one being Jesus Christ. The light of Christ is not (just) Jesus. Jesus is the Christ light.

You are connected to the light of Christ. Christ is the being. The being is Christ.

Today is a special day to honour the life of Christ. There was no life of Christ, only Christ. Christ's being is always.

The life of Christ is to epitomise and renew life itself. Life is continuous not divided.

There is only life.

A Record of Life

A Perspective of Jesus' Life by Barabbas

He shared His gifts among the people with love and light, purity and honesty, not in vain. Regardless of the tragic end it was a life well lived. His tragic end has been distorted by history. He has been made a martyr by man. People are confused by His life. The facts have been disfigured and time has corrupted His legacy.

In the name of goodness, in God He came to Earth to share the knowledge of love. That you were all made from love, are love and should act out of love for yourself and your fellow men.

Wars, greed, anger, devastation and neglect have corrupted the name of Jesus. How can one man have created such havoc? He didn't. Why has His voice been distorted with time? Why has His legacy been rewritten by man? Indoctrinated. Propaganda.

It happens today in your time. Those that have the power of love, love for the planet, face the same issues. Animals they face the enemy of man, those that do not understand.

His body is made an icon. His life of suffering taught to children. You pray at an altar. It is time for His name to be cleared. He didn't do it. He took the blame.

He took the shame. He didn't kill anyone.

He was murdered and man wants to celebrate His death, to focus on the suffering, enlarge the thinking of the mass to propagate, to feel small, suffering, to be little men, to know thy place. This is not so. It is the rising, the ascension. The spiritual uprising is bringing forward focus on the good, focus on your good, focus on life itself.

Chocolate made of poison does not warrant His joy, His life. An egg of peace? No, it is an egg of birth. Should man not listen to his own heart? The heart, an egg. So, man poisons himself with food justifying the existence of a man who brought the word of love and shone His light on the people.

My words are straight, strong and true. This is not judgement. This is truth. This is not feeble. This is strong. My rant is real. More real than your existence.

The Spirit realm is the true home. The body plays in a school of learning, called Earth. If you can play nicely, if you can progress positively on Earth, then your time on Earth was well spent and your Heaven awaits you to grow your spirit or not.

Reincarnation is real. The body is irrelevant and relevant. The spirit requires a body to play, learn and progress. Your lessons tally up. There is a book with all the lessons that count, valid to mankind. The afterlife exists. There is an existence after your life on Earth, a continuum of life.

Many have written and seen the afterlife. Many know and believe about the afterlife. Many do not understand and many do not believe and this is okay. It is not okay to abuse the image of Christ. It is not okay to celebrate His life with a cross of torture, immoral and unkind.

The rules of man have been lost in time and free will is man's gift. Man now makes up his own rules and those that are strongest rule the masses.

Individualism is on the rise. Free thought. Free morals. Free spirits are on the rise. A new ruling will take place. Man will govern himself and the strongest will lose their voices.

Truth of Self and the Collective

If Jesus had not died so tragically would man have taken notice of His teachings? There were others who taught the word of God but Jesus knew the truth. Jesus has been remembered throughout history for His teachings. His death made it so. He had more knowledge to give and more wisdom to pass on but man cut His life short.

Through His death man has only remembered part of His teachings. Through His death man has mitigated the truth, torn apart the true Jesus. Now we write through you (the writer) findings, teachings lost in the sea of propaganda, man's games.

Jesus had more enlightenment and truths to give, the truth of self and the collective. The people are my people. What did he mean?

You come as a group to learn like a team sometimes with a team leader. Your groups can be many or few or several groups working together for a cause, a purpose. Groups of souls, people collectively organising and creating.

Who is your group? Do you have a soul group? Yes, you do.

In this soul group are animals, from pets to neighbours' pets to strangers' dogs, to wild animals, to animals of the sea or air even the small insects and their friends that inhabit the earth have a part to play in the soul group, vegetation and rock too.

Mammals play a huge part in the soul group, the collective conscious. The knowledge they contain within is of importance. It seems strange and weird to your ears and even impossible but everything is possible.

The mind has become closed to the possibilities of the higher realms, the kingdom of God is vast beyond man's imagination and knowledge. It has been forgotten on entering the Earth realm but now the density of the planet is slowly lifting and the consciousness of man becoming more enlightened. There is much work to do but nevertheless man's progress is progressing.

He thirsts for knowledge of the outer worlds whilst in his human form to assist with his lessons and challenges, his writings, creations and art. The form of man is changing mentally and powerfully.

What do we mean the form of man is changing mentally and powerfully?

Man is growing in psychic powers, telepathy is becoming the norm. Again, it may not be accurate and it may be misused. It requires discipline as in everything you do. To be a master of light one is disciplined.

The thread of the power of the internet by computer is creating a psychic power and consciousness greater than man. His creation is wielding lightness and darkness. The dark will be overruled and the light will overshadow the dark but man must first go through a transition of consciousness. It is here. It is now, it is happening and the collective group of humanity as a whole is changing.

The physical power of the extended brain, the computer is shortening man's sight intellectually and physically, extending man's consciousness and shortening his ears to his own truth. The lesson of the computer is changing man's physicality and consciousness for better and for worse. Man is married to his electronic box. The few who exist without it are on the outside of man's new life, the old way.

The collective group as a whole has changed life on Earth. It has created good and bad, both are energy that is and there are the Gods of the internet, the computers that dictate to man like the church did so, the hierarchy remains. This is one example of the collective group.

It is time for man to be aware of lessons. Why did he come to Earth? Who is he working with? Who is he contracted to work with? Where will this lead?

You have choice, free will. The will of God, your higher purpose and contract is written and remains so, it is.

Man will Change

The existence of man is short lived. It is a dying breed. Seems strange and unimaginable, fiction, but what do we mean?

That man will change. He will alter his outer shell to reflect his inner shell (self). The tide is turning, the evolution of man. Why would God reflect his beauty in one form? The image of man is being rewritten.

A new prescription, hybrid. Inner thoughts will be seen, no longer hidden from view. Thought is a form of expression. Thought will be expressed externally. Thought on the inside reflected on the outside.

It takes shape in nature naturally. Man cannot hide his thought so thought must be expressed. It is already taking form in man. You will not see this in your lifetime but beyond.

Thoughts will collate and create a mass expression for good or worse. The shift is to good. Good thought. Controlled thought. Thinking out loud will be final.

Chapter 4

The Light of the Truth

Words by the Christ light

The following are a collection of stories told by the people close to Jesus of His time on Earth. In each story there is a message of truth, hope and enlightenment.

Again, there is no reference to who wrote these words. There is no other name than the light of Christ. To singularise these words does not make up the plural of the light expanding out to all from these stories.

A Little Boy Called Jesus

Once upon a time there lived a little boy called Jesus who did not know how great He was. He had many friends and His magnetic power of love attracted men, women, children, animals and all that could feel the simplicity of His love. Each felt anointed with His presence as if God had spoken to them direct and of course through the little boy Jesus, He did.

God speaks through all of you He would say, find Him within your heart, find His light, your light, find the glory of our Lord in yourself and then you will see the glory of God all around you. To look without is to look within, His words came in parables, in stories which left man searching for the truth, his own truth.

When Jesus became a teenager He too underwent the changes from boyhood to manhood and suffered the hormonal changes that take place within the physical body, but with His communion with God, the Lord gave him the power to override these changes and take the joy and delight of growing and developing into manhood.

Study the body, reflect upon its changes and accept with the growth of manhood your development in Spirit. Let the spirit grow within your body, allow it through, the more of you and Jesus did, he grew in spirit like none we had seen before on Earth.

Jesus could rise in consciousness to a state we have all yet to achieve. In His daily life He nurtured and nourished His spirit with the love of His Father. Food could fuel His body, but what will nourish and energise your spirit? The great, great consciousness can speak within you when all is still and quiet. To find peace without look within.

Many children clamoured to be his friend. They did not find him strange or out of place. They understood the spirit of the child and accepted Him as their Lord's beloved, their Lord's blessed messenger.

How many children are here on Earth today who played in the sand on the rocks with Jesus? Who laughed and talked with their friend Jesus? Many have returned to bring the message forward into another era. Children who remember their sacred and blessed moments, but some have struggled as the tortures and pain of the crucifixion mar the image of this great soul.

The lessons of the crucifixion are not to reincarnate his pain, but to love your pain and suffering as you will grow into a more beautiful world, when you accept this, pain can bring you joy. Joy is always near the end of pain. Seek the joy of life.

Joshua's Journey

In a time long ago there lived a family. Joshua was the eldest son and loved his parents very much but he knew the time had come to leave the family nest and make his own way into the world although this was not the way of his family and not what his parents wanted for him. But the young man was determined to discover new adventures in new and distant lands.

So, one day Joshua said goodbye to his tribe and his friends, took his faithful donkey and off he went heading for new adventures. Unfortunately, the stars were not aligned for this path to unfold and Joshua came upon trouble with men in the neighbouring village.

He had not long left his home when he stumbled across men murdering other men. This frightened Joshua and instead of following his instincts to go home, to know he was not ready for this venture, he continued on his path and met more men who were troubled souls and stole, they were bandits, thieves that preyed upon men's riches.

Still he continued his journey with a belly full of pride and his homeland became more distant and Joshua became lost. Eventually alone in a desert with only the campfire to give him comfort, Joshua cried, broke down and prayed to Jehovah and asked what had he done wrong?

Why had he met such terrible men and seen these awful things. God spoke to him in his heart.

'Go home my child, it is not your time to discover new lands. Stay with your family, do not be discouraged and do not listen to the whispers of others. You must know yourself more than you do now. You must not be led astray by the thoughts and opinions of others. When you choose to leave, you will know your purpose and yourself better than you do now. You will do my work and you will be more forgiving of those that have led you astray. Your time has come to be you but you must prepare for the time to leave. What you know and what you do are two different actions'.

The Sailor

A long time ago there was a sailor who loved the seas and journeyed to many lands. His name was Ella Boy and he loved to travel meeting different people with weird and wonderful customs.

His favourite was a country full of life but divided by many cultures. The sailor intermingled with the people learning many new ways to cook, to sew, to talk and to listen to your beliefs. The belief in you, in your friends and in life itself. The gift of life is treasured amongst these people. They knew their hearts and spoke with courage, the truth to all who would listen.

The sailor had been out walking soaking up the atmosphere of the market streets and its bustling activity when he noticed the beautiful lady coming out of a doorway. He couldn't see all of her face as it was partly covered by a cloth as part of her religion. But her eyes pierced his soul, spoke loudly to his heart and at once he walked towards her drawn by her hidden beauty.

The lady did not step back nor did she advance towards him, but waited patiently knowing all comes to her with times own making.

All her life the lady had known she would meet a man who loved the sea and its great mystical wonders and as he approached her she knew the love that would blossom between them would stay forever printed in the scrolls of fate.

A Wise Man

There once was a very wise man who lived in a faraway land unknown to the civilisation of his time.

This man was so wise he knew the time of day by watching the sun rise and set, he knew the seasons by nurturing the land, he knew God by listening to his heart.

The wisdom of God came to this man through his acts of kindness, his loving ways and most of all his respect for himself and all his fellow men.

One day, whilst out tending to his sheep, the wise man heard a strange sound coming from deep within the earth. He followed the sound which led him to a well hidden by trees and shrubs. There in the well was an abundance of water to feed his flock.

How had he missed this well? The times he had passed by when walking with his sheep. But the wise man knew, not until the sheep were ready to be fed would he have found water.

The Healing Hand of Jesus

Sometime long ago, there was a man named Jesus. He was revered amongst His people, He was unique with His gifts and His wise words had begun to spread throughout the land.

Who was this mystic? Where had He come from? And why was He here? The people questioned His authority. He was beloved and travelled far and wide the ancient land.

His story began to unfold with a fight in a market town between two men. He had the ability to quieten their angry hearts and calm their minds. With a gesture and a look that removed the thorn stuck in their throats, the men were quietened and sorry for hurting the other. The men fell to their knees in forgiveness and vowed to each other never to harm the other again.

This was not to be. As time moved forward, the old wound had not healed and the angst between the men rose up again. This time with more fury till one of the men lay still, unable to move. His heart had stopped, he no longer spoke and the breath had gone out of his chest. His friend lay next to him sobbing and full of remorse.

When Jesus passed through the market town again, He heard of this story and went to seek out the man who had killed his friend. Jesus lay His hands on this man and blessed him.

You will work with me but not in this lifetime in another where my words and healing can be spread through numbers. You will learn true forgiveness but there will be one who will ride your tail and test your ability to forgive. If you can overcome your burden and rise up in true forgiveness, I will walk beside you through each lifetime and guide you, be with you and you will know my heart. This is important as you will become one with God and in doing so lift the hearts of men.

The man felt the healing light once more, this time enter deep within his chest wall and he began to sob for the friend he had lost and had loved so much. Jesus promised him the eternal love of his friend and guaranteed that with his faith to control himself, he would become an enlightened one and his word would be sung on men's lips.

Jesus gently kissed the top of this man's head and asked, trust in me as I trust in you, love me as I love you, call out to me and I will be there. Take my healing and give it out to those that need me. Keep your lips closed to the day I ask you to write and know your seat in Heaven will be to rest with the enlightened ones. You will go unnoticed amongst your earthly men till the day I call upon you and a new door shall open and I will walk with you.

As Jesus walked away, this man knew with all of his heart the pledge was sealed, his fate drawn in the stars and mourned less each day for his friend and gave out love and kindness to each man he met, seeing his friends face in every smile. His anger and remorse lessened, he began to take control of his heart and he knew he was blessed, at one with his old friend and new friend Jesus.

Jesus kept His promise as foretold and the brothers became one. Even though till this day the lesson continues between the souls, the burden is eased and they are helped by the enlightened ones. Jesus walks beside 'the fighter' now 'the lover' of men and a new journey is about to start. In the house of God, they will find peace and true forgiveness will be learnt.

To forgive thyself is not enough, to control thyself is everything and everything is in order and everything is.

Trust in Jesus

One day when Jesus was out walking amongst His people, He noticed a little girl sitting by a well crying and lonely. He stopped and asked her name. Isabelle, the little girl said as her tears started to dry. She felt the comforting voice change the moment from fear to love.

Why do you cry, my child? Jesus asked.

My mother has been killed and my father has left town. I am all alone. I have no brothers or sisters and I have nowhere to go. My home has been taken over by another family and they took all our belongings. I live in the street and I'm poor. I have no shoes and my friends mock me. My father's friends do not want to know me and my mother didn't have any family. I feel alone and I'm scared. I'm hungry and thirsty and need a bed to rest my head. I'm so tired and weary.

Can you help me? The little girl asked Jesus.

Of course, I can. Do you trust me?

Yes, I can see God in your eyes and I know you have been brought to me to help me with my lessons.

Then follow me, my child, I know a woman who will love you, clothe you, feed you and give you a good life.

Chapter 5

The Light of the Rose

Words by the Higher realms of Spirit

The following words are given from the higher realms of Spirit close to Jesus to assist those unfolding their spiritual abilities, to give direction and comfort on the Earthly plane and further understanding of the Spirit world.

Finally, the closing words of the Epilogue by Jesus is to reassure those in need that you are not alone and you have only to ask and we will assist you on your journey.

The Inner Light

In amongst a rose bush are thorns, which do you see, the beautiful rose in bud, blossoming, in bloom fully open to the sun and rain having grown to its full potential, utterly beautiful with the most delightful scent, a fragrance to endure.

Or, the thorns hidden discretely along the stem, overshadowed by the green leaves, catching you out if you are not careful when you hold the rose.

It is a joy, a vision of delicate beauty. The spontaneity is missing, it is perfectly shaped. Divine in its essence, but what do you see the thorn or the rose?

Your Heart

In your heart lies all the answers to your questions.

How to listen to your heart is difficult to the untrained ear. Train your ear to hear your heart. Let your heart speak to your ears.

An inner knowing, an inner glowing, an inner feeling of belief and joy will lead you to your destiny.

Let your heart speak, speak from the heart.

Earthly Matters

You are connected to Earth through your physical body, to Spirit through your spiritual body and God via your soul.

Let the light of your soul shine brightly. Do not let the earthly matters bring you down or dim your light.

Spirit of Man

The spirit of man is on different levels. On Earth you are all together.

In Spirit you separate to where you belong. These levels are at different pitches some high, some low, different frequencies.

There's a lot you can't see in Spirit as on Earth or any other planet with life.

Inner Peace

Inner peace is a knowing in your heart that you are the spark of God, the light made light.

You are not of this mortal world, you are immortal.

Your spirit carries your soul
Your body carries your spirit
Your heart is all knowing.

Wonders of all Worlds

Open your heart to the wonders of all worlds to mankind and beyond.

The animal world derives from beyond this world. The origin of the species is not of this world (Earth).

You inhabit the Earth then you will return to a place called Spirit. The Spirit world and its inhabitants are varied from higher worlds to lower worlds vibrating at varying frequencies.

The Responsibility of Man

When men sit together in goodness, in light, in prayer, in love and heal and bless, this is a beautiful thing. They carry the goodness with them and continue their work wherever they go. They are responsible, they know the cause and effect of their actions, they are enlightened.

Think through each action. Thinking is good. Good thought. There is also the beautiful spontaneous action. The action of spirit.

The Divine Path

Take the divine path and follow your heart in all that you do.

If the path eludes you then wait for it to open to you. Stay awake in your being to be shown the way.

I know my soul
I know my way
I know what I am meant to do and
I follow the divine path.

Everything in Balance

Everything in balance. There is wanting and there is over wanting.

Greed is indulgence, ignorance of self. Ignoring the balance within oneself. Whether it is food or materialism, greed is rife on the planet.

We are not talking of denying your right to abundance, this is your birthright. But, for example, to ignore the balance of good food to stimulate, nourish, fuel the body is ignorance. Over eating is on the rise. Under eating without purpose is negligent, under eating with purpose is obsessive.

Finding balance in all things is good for the soul to keep a balance. Each soul's balance is different. Knowing your soul's balance is important.

Discipline

Practising your art takes discipline. Discipline of the earthly self, discipline of the higher self. All needs discipline.

Control and a knowing. How to control the heart? With the will of God, Trust.

How to control the lower self?

Love it, nurture it, don't abuse it, be it and let it, the lower self, have a voice in your life.

A whisper.

Courage

We can bring courage to you, or you can find courage in you, or you can know and be courageous.

We suggest the knowing comes first to be courageous. Do not deplete your energy searching for the courage. If you know something to be right, follow your instincts. This is courage.

When you are given a task and you feel weakened by a situation, stay still. Gather the momentum, be at peace. Drop it and let the divine intervene and sing to you at the right time and in your renewed energy, in divine alignment, let go of the fear, the fear now redundant, act and in this action, it is easy. It is.

Courage is knowing, an act of faith in you.

Take Hold of Your Emotions

Frustration, anger, irritation do not serve you. If you are frustrated do nothing, let it pass. Take hold of your emotions. The frustration is counterproductive.

To take hold of your emotions is to let go, walk away, if necessary remove yourself from a situation. 'Get a grip' means do not let your energy go into another's, a drama, an unwanted debate, it is easier to stay self-contained then to lose yourself.

Communication is necessary to unfold thought but if you do not desire to communicate then don't, but let it go. Do not ingest unwanted thoughts. How to let go? It's simple, focus on something you want, you love, you like and forget it ever existed. Do not give it life.

We do not suggest you ignore important issues that you must face, but find the right tone, the right voice, the truth and the ease to deal with your matter. To be at one with you will make the realisation of self easier to be expressed, the expression of you.

Love of Life

Life is about love, to find love in your life, not only in others but in you.

Do you love who you are? Do you have time to replenish, 'smell the roses' be who you are? If not, then find the time to spend with you.

It is important to be you. Life will unfold in harmony. Please you as you. Love who you are. Embrace your gifts, your character, your uniqueness. Emphasise you are a child of God, an extension of Source, a divine spark, a spirit of light, a product of the Universe.

This time is yours to learn, to grow and to enjoy the little things, the big events, the company.

Does life please you?

Inner Strength

When you feel heavy, burdened, overwhelmed or anxious with life's trials, your lessons; ask for the light to shine and have faith, trust the help you seek, the love surrounds you.

Take your nose away from the window pane, stand back and let the door be opened from the other side.

In time of pain, reach inside of you and find the inner strength God has given you. An abundance of energy in your heart. Tap into the reservoir of life, divine life, earthly energy and accept your choices and fears, situations and be you.

Do not fold into the situation, pull on the reservoir of life. Answers, knowings, dreams, signs all real. A nudge here and voice from nowhere, you will be guided.

We have great love for humanity. Let us help you on your path.

Being Open

Are you open to healing?
Are you open to receiving love?
Are you open to life blossoming?

Being open like the rose in full bloom to sunlight, nourishment, petals for bees, a feast for the eyes, beauty in abundance, the smell of sweet perfume, the soft touch of the flower.

Are you open to the rain cleansing your being?

It is important to open the heart to be a channel of love and inspiration.

When the heart closes its petals it resists life's joys, the sweetness sours and the light grows dim.

Be open to the light in your being, the being of you connecting to the light of your creator, the light shining all around you.

Christmas Truth

Christmas Cheer
Christmas Joy
Christmas Love

Christmas a time for giving
Christmas a time for spending
Christmas a time for repent

Reflect and repent
Where do you repent?
What do you repent?
With whom do you repent?
Find the answers within

Reflect and repeat
Repeat in your mind times of joy
Repeat in your mind times of cheer
Repeat and repent no more

To repent is to forgive
To forgive is to accept
To accept is to tolerate
To tolerate is to love.

Truth

Speak the truth
Know the truth
Be the truth.

Let the truth flow from your voice and mind.

We speak here of the God light, the truth in self. Not the truth of a situation or the truth of man's games. Turn the light on any situation and you will be given the answer. You hold your own torch.

The Truth Within

The gender of love is insignificant in the realms of Spirit. Spirit know love in its purest form and are blessed with the gift of free will. So, Spirit makes the choices man has been given.

Why wait till death us do part? Why wait till the promised land to fulfill those promises? Bring Heaven to Earth for all to see.

Love is not blind, it is clear and in its truest form simple. Look for the truth within.

Be the Joy

We have joy, you have joy
Joy is in us, we are joy

Write joy, see joy
Look for joy, feel joy
Taste joy, be joy
You are joy

The light of joy is golden
Wear the golden light
Be the golden light
Radiate light from inside out

Let it reflect in your work
In your words, in your attire
In your house, everywhere, your garden
Be the joy

Christ is joy
Jesus knows joy of the heart
Take it into your heart
The joy of healing, the healing joy.

Come to Me

The throne is empty the land is barren
nobody at the helm.
Darkness rules and man run riot
killing each other for money.
The purse is wicked, the good will say
trust in the Lord for He will provide.

Those that steal will know theft themselves.
Those that lie will never know the truth
and those that belittle other men
are small in themselves.

Those that know peace give out love
and receive love of their fellow men.
Those that know riches of the land
will give out plenty and grow with their crops.

But those who are cruel and murder and pillage
are dissatisfied with who they are
lost in their own mental mind.
The voices of doom speak to them loudly
and greed is rife.

Until the white rose in the centre of their being
accepts who they are and the true love of Christ
the true love of themselves
and the true word of their light
they will no longer know
the goodness man has to offer
the love they can cherish
the joy of their beauty.

They cripple themselves lost in their minds
a desert of grey cloud and a sickness in the soul.

Come to me I ask
let me lay my hand upon your head
heal the heart and give you bread.

Come to me I ask
let me show you the light
to heal your mind
free your spirit
and show you love in kind.

Come to me I ask of you
step forward to the light
ask no more of yourself
and let me take the weight.

I give you my love
I give you my honour
I give you all that I am.

In me is you
and we will be the light of you as two.

I'll take your hand
lay out your path
with a steady foot for you to walk.

Slowly your life will change each day
and I'll be beside you every step of the way.

Epilogue

The Light of The Way

Words by Jesus

Enjoy your time on the planet Earth and if life gets you down, causes you distress, brings you upset and you lose your peace, then this prayer written in the light given to the channel, I give back to you to know I am always here for each and every one.

I am the light and I will light your way.

A Prayer to Christ

Today is the day
I shall rise and leave my troubles
at the door of Christ

He shall uplift my troubled heart
Take away my burdens

Help me give to Him my weary spirit

I will see more clearly through His light
I will know more dearly His love

Through Him I shall be restored
With love I shall give out the light

I am one with Him and believe
my life is divincly guided.

With Love and Light

Take these words into the light as in each word your voice will be heard by the higher realms of Spirit and those that require assistance will be shown the way.

Your thoughts are like a voice in the Spirit world. We can hear you think and we know your thoughts of good intentions. Thoughts have power and the power can be of no consequence or of consequence.

You do have privacy, but your actions are known. Your innermost private thoughts are valued as your own but as you rise in consciousness you will know all thought forms are transparent. They have power, controlled thought has power. Power to create, manifest and be. Effect and affect others in the world around you or away from you. Be careful what you think, a child has the gift of play, an adult has the gift of thought and play.

We leave you with our thoughts of love and light.

Quick Search Guide

D

Death 5, 51, 52, 66, 73, 77, 79, 118

Discipline 15, 23, 26, 43, 81, 110

Divine 9, 13, 15, 36, 61, 70, 73, 101, 108, 111, 113, 114

E

Earth 15, 29, 59, 104

Emotions 10, 12, 13, 22, 50, 71, 112

Energy ii-iii, 12, 16, 18, 21, 22, 23, 29, 43, 49, 61-63, 64, 66, 68, 81, 111, 112, 114

Enlightenment 29, 50, 79, 85

Entity 61, 66, 75

Eternal 9, 47, 68, 95

F

Family 20, 23, 23-24, 25, 36, 37, 40, 42, 45, 71

Forgive 43-45, 96, 116

Forgiveness 14, 43

G

Gift(s) 7, 20-21, 36, 38, 41, 45, 56, 60, 71-72, 76, 113, 118, 129

Growth i, 26, 28, 44

H

Happy 18, 37, 38, 44, 55

Harmony 12, 14, 16-17, 42, 113

Healing 5, 23-24, 42, 51, 54, 62, 69, 94-95, 115, 119

Heart i, 3, 13, 27, 29, 43, 56, 66, 69, 74, 77, 90, 93, 102, 105, 106, 108, 110, 114, 115, 122, 27

Heaven 11, 14, 18, 22, 27, 44, 59, 68, 77, 95, 118

Holy 5, 35-36, 40, 64, 73

Honour 6, 61, 71, 75, 123

About RoseAnne

RoseAnne Rosslin has been communicating with Spirit from an early age and is a channel and a medium who is known for her ability to help others develop their spiritual gifts. She has given many channellings to help them on their course, offering comfort and evidence of Spirit.

Through many years working with Spirit with her natural gift as a medium, these words have been given to RoseAnne from the Christ realm. RoseAnne has collated the channelled text over twenty years and has been guided by the Christ realm to produce her first book 'The Light of Jesus'.

Further Information

RoseAnne Rosslin continues to write on behalf of the Higher realms of Spirit and from the Christ realm. If you would like to be notified of the inspired writings, please subscribe at:

www.roseannerosslin.com

Printed in Poland
by Amazon Fulfillment
Poland Sp. z o.o., Wrocław